KT-142-102

# The McGraw-Hill Film Viewer's Guide

David Bordwell
*University of Wisconsin*

Boston   Burr Ridge, IL   Dubuque, IA   Madison, WI   New York   San Francisco   St. Louis
Bangkok   Bogotá   Caracas   Lisbon   London   Madrid
Mexico City   Milan   New Delhi   Seoul   Singapore   Sydney   Taipei   Toronto

The McGraw-Hill Film Viewer's Guide
David Bordwell

Published by McGraw-Hill, an imprint of the McGraw-Hill Companies, Inc., 1221
Avenue of the Americas, New York, NY 10020. Copyright © 2001 by the McGraw-Hill
Companies, Inc. All rights reserved.
No part of this publication may be reproduced or distributed in any form or by any means,
or stored in a database or retrieval system, without the prior written consent of The
McGraw-Hill Companies, Inc., including, but not limited to, in any network or other
electronic storage or transmission, or broadcast for distance learning.

1 2 3 4 5 6 7 8 9 0 2CUS/2CUS 0 9 8 7 6 5 4 3 2 1 0

ISBN 0-07-238824-2

www.mhhe.com

# C O N T E N T S

This manual supplements *Film Art: An Introduction* by discussing two aspects of film appreciation. First, the manual considers how to watch films with more understanding, and then it examines how to express your views of films through various kinds of writing. In addition, the manual offers tips on going beyond the textbook to explore the world of cinema on your own.

# *Watching Films*

## ▼ What to Watch For

### The Whole Film

*Film Art* emphasizes that to appreciate a movie you have to consider it as a whole. Some parts may be intriguing in themselves, but the film operates as a total system, and any part gains its full meaning in that context. This is why we introduce the concepts of overall form (Part Two) and style (Part Four). Whether you're watching a film for diversion or for deeper understanding, as part of an evening's entertainment or as a class assignment, you'll appreciate the film most fully if you have an overall sense of how it's put together. This means developing the habit of thinking of any part, no matter how small, in relation to the rest of the film.

For example, two lines of dialogue from *Jerry Maguire* have entered everyday American English. "Show me the money!" has become a cliché, while "You complete me" has been parodied in comedy skits. Taken by themselves, they are easy to mock. In the overall film, however, they play complicated roles. "Show me the money!" is at first an amusing line which Rod Tidwell uses to make Jerry swear he'll serve as a good agent for him. Rod wants to amass money to keep his family secure in the years when he can no longer play football. This is a businesslike attitude, but we've already seen that one side of Jerry doesn't want the sports business to be wholly about money. He has glimpsed the possibility of actually serving his clients as friends. So even though Jerry agrees to help Rod get a bigger paycheck, we can anticipate

a conflict coming up. As the plot develops, Rod will learn that his search
for bigger paychecks demands that he think not only of himself and his
family but his team.

"You complete me" first appears when Jerry and Dorothy have quit
the firm they work for and watch a loving deaf-mute couple sign to each
other. Dorothy knows American Sign Language and can interpret their
gestures—a piece of knowledge which tells us that she's a sympathetic
person. More generally, the line works as a summation of both Dorothy's
and Jerry's situations. She is moved by his "mission statement," which
shows that her idealism finds an outlet in his dream of a personalized
sports agency. Jerry, on the other hand, must come to understand what
Dorothy brings to him. He loves her son and she has bolstered his
confidence, but he is not ready to love her fully. Dorothy guides him
toward becoming, in her words, "the man he almost is." By the end of the
film, when he declares "You complete me" in front of a room full of
women with unhappy relationships, he admits that he needs her to fulfil the
best side of himself. As with "Show me the money!" the line gains its
deepest meaning in the overall development of the plot.

The overall context of a movie can make any element significant.
Consider credit sequences. At a minimum, credits can set a mood, like an
overture in an opera or stage musical. The thunderous, looming title
credit of *Terminator 2: Judgment Day* is stamped in flame-licked steel
plates that slowly enlarge while metallic percussion hammers out a
frantic pulse. The shot evokes the flames of nuclear war, the danger of
physical action, a battle against machines, and the film's concern with
humanizing its cyborg. By contrast, as we point out in *Film Art* (p. 387),
the candybox credits of *Meet Me in St. Louis* evoke nostalgia for cozy
family life at the turn of the century. For *Se7en*, David Fincher wanted to
set up anxiety in the spectator from the start, especially since the villain
appears rather late in the film, so he commissioned graphic designer Kyle
Cooper to create fast-cut, scratch-and-burn credits which suggest
mutilation and madness.

# At the Very Start: Logos and Opening Credits

Most theatrical motion pictures begin in a standardized way. First are the logos identifying the distributor and the production company. The major distributors have logos known around the world–the Paramount mountain, the MGM lion, Columbia's Lady Liberty, the Warner Bros. shield, the Universal globe, and the enormous futuristic letters of Twentieth Century Fox. The production company responsible for the film also tries to present a vivid, memorable image, as when Spielberg's Amblin Company recycles the silhouette of the bicycle against the moon from *ET*. In addition, an introductory logo can play a formal, stylistic, or thematic role in the film. The Paramount peak dissolves into a real mountain at the beginning of *Raiders of the Lost Ark*, and in the opening of *The Matrix* the Warners shield loses its bright blue and yellow tones and becomes a gloomy circuit-board green suitable for the cyberspace adventure which follows. Until the 1950s, a feature film followed a set format: lengthy credits at the very start, a "The End" title at the close, often followed by a shot listing cast members and their roles. In the 1950s, some films began to have "precredits" sequences, one or two scenes which whetted the viewer's interest before the opening credits. Later filmmakers hit upon one strategy that's still common: Start the plot immediately but present the credits superimposed over the action we see, as in *Jerry Maguire*.

For many decades the credits listed were quite selective. Nearly all of the hundreds of workers who participated in making the film were long-term studio employees, and so they went uncredited. When studios became chiefly distribution companies in the 1960s and 1970s, all workers, from stars down to carpenters and grips, became freelance workers, and they were able to negotiate a credit line. Now everyone who works on the movie, in any capacity, must be credited by name. As a result, a new format arose. The opening credits (also called the "main title") lists key personnel: main stars, screenwriters, cinematographer, composer, special-effects creators, editors, producers, and–last by tradition–director. The full credits (or "end title") rolls at the film's conclusion, almost always in small white type on a black background. For the major participants, the size, sequence, and placement of the credits are negotiated contractually.

Credits can also anticipate motifs that will arise in the film's story. Several of Hitchcock's films had credits designed by Saul Bass, who had a genius for finding a graphic design to epitomize aspects of the film. Bass created the spiraling opening imagery of *Vertigo,* which introduces the motif of vision (an enlarged eye) and the hero's fear of falling (the sinister tower). Bass filled the opening frames of *North by Northwest* with crosshatched parallels, which first evoke latitude and longitude lines (this movie will be about traveling) and then become the grid of a New York City skyscraper's facade. Bass's simpler horizontal credits for *Psycho*, blocks of white zipping on and offscreen against a black background, anticipate the window blinds and the highway line markers of the film's first part. Kyle Cooper's credits for *Mission Impossible* also anticipate upcoming action, sandwiching names among a flurry of images which will be seen later in the film, all introducing key elements of treachery and romance. (It's as if the credits sequence became a trailer for the movie.) Less strenuous are the witty opening credits of *The Thomas Crown Affair* (1999) where letters swap places, hinting at how Crown will pull off his heist.

Similarly, end credits can participate in the overall film. The closing titles of *Armageddon* are wedged into home-video-style footage of the young couple's wedding, a scene which brings the plot to a close. *A Bug's Life* charmed audiences with its final credits, which parodied the "NG" ("No Good," or blooper) shots that used to accompany comedies. And some filmmakers cunningly add material *after* the final credits, as if rewarding devoted viewers who didn't rush for the exit. *Airplane!* was one of the first films to save a gag for the very end of the credits, a device exploited by John Hughes in several films. Takeshi Kitano, by contrast, adds a lyrical landscape shot to the final credits for *Sonatine,* softening the harshness of the plot's last scene. Each part of a film, even its very first or very last moments, can contribute to its overall effect.

# Where to Watch

## The Theater Experience

Part of the pleasure of movies is the very experience of going out to a movie theater. "I like to stand in line like everyone else," says Steven Spielberg, "because that creates anticipation. Buying the popcorn and the soft drinks heightens the anticipation." The presence of other moviegoers can also make a weak movie enjoyable. "If the audience likes it and you don't," Spielberg points out, "they'll encourage you to see beyond your own prejudices and enjoy it more than you would if you saw it alone." Comedies particularly benefit from a large audience. On video *There's Something about Mary* can seem sluggish, but when seen with a crowd it can elicit virtually nonstop laughter.

For most of film history, the feature was only one part of the show. The feature was accompanied by newsreels, scientific films, comedy shorts (featuring stars like the Three Stooges and the Little Rascals), cartoons, and even live acts. In the 1930s, American theaters held contests and giveaways, sometimes interrupting the movie for a stage show. Television changed all that by providing news, cartoons, variety shows, quiz programs, and educational documentaries for free. By the 1970s, theatrical movies were accompanied by very few extras. There might be local advertisements, commercials for national brands like Coca-Cola, and a brief introductory film promoting the exhibition chain to which the theater belonged. There would, however, always be short films announcing other features playing in town or soon to arrive. Audiences call these "coming attractions" or "previews," while the industry calls them "trailers" (because they used to "trail" the feature).

Today producing a trailer for a mainstream Hollywood release can cost half a million dollars. Why is this a good investment? Because trailers are central to marketing the film. They target people who have already shown themselves to be moviegoers. The trailer can also be aimed directly at certain tastes, so a horror movie can be accompanied by a trailer for an upcoming horror release. Very often, exhibitors are obliged to show a trailer for a film from the distributor which supplied the feature. The Artisan company piggybacked several trailers onto the prints of *The Blair Witch Project*, so that film's success helped promote upcoming Artisan releases.

There are two kinds of trailers. One is called a "teaser" because it is very short—perhaps only thirty seconds—and gives the audience only a hint about the film. There might be a few shots, atmospheric music, and the film's logo, as well as a Web address. Some teasers include specially shot footage that won't appear in the film. Not wanting to reveal the dinosaurs of *Jurassic Park,* Spielberg shot a teaser depicting the discovery of the dinosaur DNA during a mining expedition; it ends with a glowing shot of a mosquito trapped in amber. Teasers, which are most common for U.S. summer releases, may appear several months before the film opens.

The standard trailer runs two or three minutes. Even though it is usually cut very fast, it tries to give a fuller sense of the film than a teaser does. It identifies the stars, points up the genre the film belongs to, and sketches story lines. Sometimes trailers supply too much: Many moviegoers complain that trailers now give away important plot twists.

Trailers are assembled out of alternative takes from the shooting stage, so they usually aren't the exact same shots you'll see in the finished film. Sometimes a trailer's images and lines of dialogue don't end up in the film as released, because last-minute changes have altered them. Music, one of the last elements of postproduction, is seldom fully represented in the trailer, which may use generic background music or some easily available classics. (*Carmina Burana* is a favorite.) Similarly, since most special-effects shots are finished quite late in the production, a trailer may lack many of the film's visual splendors.

Trailers intensify the anticipation which Spielberg identifies as so central to the moviegoing experience. *Star Wars* fans attended *Meet Joe Black* again and again just to watch the trailer for *The Phantom Menace,* so the trailer helped *Meet Joe Black*'s business. George Lucas, knowing that some fans would try to buy or steal the trailer, insisted that theaters that didn't return the trailers wouldn't be shipped the feature! Trailers are so much a part of the theater experience that DVD releases now routinely include trailers as an extra attraction; there's always interest in seeing what scenes were selected and how the movie was sold.

## Home Video

*Film Art* discusses the differences between film on film and film on video versions in two places (pp. 15–17 and 214). There's little to add here, but we can make some recommendations:

1.  When renting or buying a video version, avoid "pan-and-scan" versions. Opt instead for the letterboxed video version, which should be identified on the box. If an opening title declares, "This version

has been formatted to fit your TV," you will not be seeing a letterboxed version.

2.   Some North American video rental chains, notably Blockbuster, often refuse to carry a film unless producers supply a version which eliminates sexual or violent material that was in the theatrical release. These softer versions are usually not labeled as such and may significantly alter dialogue, music, and the images. They aren't reliable for purposes of film study, and even for casual viewing you should search out the original theatrical version.

3.   A film on video may be available in a "director's cut." Both it and the original release are valid versions of the movie. The original was what audiences saw at the time, and so it has historical significance, but the director's cut is what the filmmaker would have preferred us to see. In some cases, as in *Blade Runner*, the differences can be substantial. If you are writing about the film, try to see both versions and specify in your piece which one you're concentrating on. Unhappily, it's not always possible to see both versions; in some cases, as with *Close Encounters of the Third Kind*, directors' cuts have replaced the original theatrical versions.

4.   Keep in mind as you watch a video version that it is pictorially quite different from the original theatrical film. As a rule, color and lighting will be significantly brighter than in the film print. Muted or grayer color schemes will look more saturated. Shadow areas will tend to go solid black, whereas in the original film they will darken gradually. Reds may flare. On DVDs, edges may be oversharp and soft textures may acquire a harder look. DVDs also may create digital artifacts, such as "tiling" during fast action or blooming purples within areas of solid black.

5.   If at all possible, try to see the film on the theater screen before seeing it on video!

## Movies on the Internet

Some films have been available on the Internet since the late 1990s, but the corner was turned in  1999 with a rush of innovations. Short downloadable movies became available on Ifilm and Atomfilm; Sightsound.com provided the first rentable digital feature (the independent $\pi$); fans posted  pirated copies of *The Phantom Menace* and *The Matrix*; and the first film was produced for Internet distribution (*The Quantum Project*). In early 2000 several companies were gearing up to distribute motion pictures through broadband net access, which speeds up browsing and provides higher-quality video imagery. And as television monitors become connected to the Internet, people will not be watching only on computer screens.

Digital video suffers many of the problems of analog video, but it will doubtless improve in quality. Some commentators, such as the critic Roger Ebert, predict that movies via the Internet will fundamentally change how Hollywood does business by creating a new level of exhibition. A studio might choose to release a film simultaneously to theaters and to the Net, offering Net access for a lower price--a bit like publishing both paperback and hardcover versions of a novel at the same time. A viewer who saw the film on the Net and liked it might well decide to go see it in a theater for the full experience. Perhaps some marginal films would be released only to the Net, the way some books are published only in paperback. In any case, films made for the Net or released via the Net will still have those qualities of form, style, and theme displayed in theatrical films.

### Internet Movie Sites

Any list of Internet sites can quickly become obsolete, but here are some outstanding sites offering films for rent or for free.

**atomfilms.com** Animated films and shorts available for rental or viewing on the Web.

**dfilm.com** Independent and experimental shorts.

**ifilm.com** Independent shorts.

**mdle.com/ClassicFilms** Silent films.

**mediatrip.com** A vast array of features, short films, music videos, and interviews with filmmakers.

**reeluniverse.com** Short films.

**rivalquest.com/super8** Super-8mm films.

**rs6.loc.gov/papr/mpixhome** Silent films from the U.S. Library of Congress.

**shortbuzz** Independent shorts.

**shortends.com** Short films.

**sightsound.com** Classic and offbeat contemporary features and shorts.

**thenewvenue.com** Independent and experimental shorts.

**Yahoo!Broadcast** Silent films, experimental, low-budget classics.

## Local Film Culture

Don't become so dependent on suburban multiplexes, home video, and
your modem that you neglect to look around your community. Many
cities and towns, as well as college campuses, have a stimulating local
film culture. It takes no more than a glance at a newspaper to discover
exciting cinema activities taking place around you.

   **Student groups**. Student government, academic departments, or
interest groups enrich campuses with films and visiting speakers. Alumni
or alumnae who have found success in the film industry may return to
talk about their work. If your campus doesn't have a group bringing the
films you want to see, why not start one?

   **Museums and art centers** often have continuing film programs,
usually screening on weekends. Many of these institutions have become
world-famous for giving audiences access to hard-to-see cinema. The
Film Center at the School of the Art Institute of Chicago, for instance,
has a tradition of screening films from Hong Kong and Iran. The Institute
for Contemporary Art in London plays host to extraordinary programs of
experimental cinema. Toronto's Cinémathèque Ontario, Philadelphia's
Museum of Contemporary Art, Harvard's Film Archive, the American
Cinémathèque of Los Angeles, the Pacific Film Archive in Berkeley,
London's National Film Theatre of the British Film Institute—these and
many other centers provide viewers a feast of films and filmmakers.

   **Festivals**. You may not be able to jet into Sundance (late January),
Cannes (mid-May), or Venice (late August), but there are over 500 other
annual showcases of unusual filmmaking, and some probably take place
near you. Toronto, Montreal, Vancouver, Chicago, New York, San
Francisco, Miami, Austin, Seattle, Fort Lauderdale, and many other
North American cities hold large annual festivals. So do cities in England
(London, Cambridge, Sheffield, Manchester), Scotland (Edinburgh),
Ireland (Dublin, Cork), New Zealand (Auckland, Wellington), and
Australia (Brisbane, Melbourne, Sydney). Europe, Asia, Africa, and
Latin America host dozens of others. Many cities are getting into the act.
You can attend festivals in Charleston, South Carolina; Bradford, U.K.;
Athens, Georgia; Indianapolis, Indiana; Calgary, Canada; Darlinghurst,
Australia; Maitland, Florida; and Madison, Wisconsin.

   Often festivals focus on a theme or genre. There are festivals
devoted to animation, fantasy and science fiction, film noir ("Shots in the
Dark" in Nottingham, U.K.), Asian culture, African culture, first-time
directors,  gay and lesbian life, documentaries, the environment, human

rights, experimental film, and film restoration. There's even a festival for films rejected by other festivals (The Rough and Ruined Film Festival, held in Amsterdam, Vancouver, and Minneapolis every summer). Whatever your film tastes, there are probably festivals addressing them.

Film festivals carry the excitement of moviegoing to a high pitch. Audiences are enthusiastic, often cheering brand-new releases or recent restorations. Filmmakers show up to answer questions, and most are approachable. Innumerable friendships have been forged while standing on line for a late-night festival screening.

You can learn about festivals you might visit from Adam Langer's *Film Festival Guide* (Chicago: Chicago Review Press, 1998) and Chris Gore's *Ultimate Film Festival Survival Guide* (Los Angeles: Lone Eagle, 1999). For up-to-the-minute information on festival dates in your neighborhood, check the calendar prepared by *Variety* at <www.variety.com>.

The best single source of information about world film culture—festivals, archives, awards, books, film schools, and national cinemas—is the annual *Variety International Film Guide*, edited by Peter Cowie.

 # How to Watch

### Developing Memory and Taking Notes

The entirety of *Film Art* is devoted to showing you what to watch for in a film, but if you intend to write something about it, you will want to watch with particular concentration. One strategy is to start to develop a *film memory*. Some people are naturally endowed with an ability to recall lines of dialogue, but anyone can increase what she or he retains from experiencing a movie. You can decide to notice certain aspects of film technique. For instance, as the movie starts, you can set out to notice particular kinds of shots; you can become, we might say, "shotconscious."

For example, once you decide to watch for camera movement in *Titanic*, you'll quickly notice the various ways in which James Cameron uses it. The camera follows Rose and Jack along the deck, it tracks in to someone to underline a facial expression, and it pursues the captain as he helplessly wades into his flooding bridge. Having noticed camera movement throughout the movie, you'll be more likely to register the impact of the film's final shot. The camera glides through the wreckage, which morphs into the promenade deck as it was before the crash, and the shot becomes the young Rose's optical point of view as she floats into the salon and up the stairs to take Jack's hand (itself a motif throughout the film). As the camera separates from her optical point of view, it tilts up to the light streaming through the dome. The one long take carries us from the present to the past, from the reality of the sunken ship to Rose's dream world—one which, the song suggests, she visits every night. This extravagant long take shows the couple perpetually young, reunited beyond death.

Some people say that watching for technique distracts them from the story, and it is true that many movies try not to call attention to their style. But you can learn to watch for both technique and story. It's multitasking, like driving a car while carrying on a conversation. It just takes practice.

Still, at any moment a lot is going on in a movie; it's hard to watch for everything at once. That's why it's good to concentrate on certain elements. In addition, if you want to study a movie, either for writing or just in order to deepen your understanding, you'll want to watch it several times. We all know how the movies we love reveal unexpected pleasures on repeated viewings. A scene you didn't much care for becomes a new favorite, and fine points of plot or performance stand out when you know what's coming up next.

Repeated viewings are essential if you plan to write about the film, and so is note taking. Because movies are dense with all kinds of visual and sonic information, notes help you recall key points. How do you take notes? If you're watching the film on video, no problem; you can stop, reverse, and replay as much as you like. Sometimes, though, you'll have to write during a screening. Here you shouldn't aim for perfect penmanship, since you're the only person who'll have to decipher your scratches. Try writing without lifting your eyes from the screen; you'll be surprised how legible the results can be. You may want to use a light-tipped pen (available in office supply stores), which casts a small beam on the page to guide your writing without disturbing others.

But, you're probably asking, if I can't capture everything, what do I take notes on? That depends on your writing project, which is the subject of the next section of this manual.

# *Writing about Films*

You'll typically encounter three sorts of writing assignment in an introductory film course. A short **screening report** asks you to demonstrate your understanding of a film and its relationship to a course topic. It's somewhat like an essay answer on an examination. Another type of assignment is the film **review**, which lets you try writing the sort of evaluative commentary you might find in *Newsweek* or *Rolling Stone*. Third, there is the **analytical essay,** a longer piece which digs more deeply and develops a sustained argument about the film. The analytical essay is the longest, most complicated, and (for most students) the most challenging writing assignment.

## The Screening Report

A screening report usually runs one to two double-spaced pages. Your purpose here is to demonstrate a general familiarity with the film and to show that you understand its relevance to a course topic. You should think of writing two to five paragraphs which develop a single aspect of the film, using examples from your notes.

For instance, suppose that the course is currently studying film genre, and the assignment asks you to submit a screening report pointing out aspects of *Halloween* which make it typical of the horror film. In a page or two, you can develop only two or three main points, so you should select what is most central to the reading, lectures, and discussions in the course at that point. Suppose that the course has focused on genre conventions. You could then pick out three aspects of *Halloween* that rely on horror conventions. You might focus on the nature of the monster, the structure of the plot, and the treatment of the female protagonist.

For each of these points you could develop a solid paragraph. Michael Myers, the slasher-figure, might seem to be a mortal man, but he is unstoppable by knives, bullets, and a two-story fall. He seems to fit the definition of a monster as a creature with powers not explainable by ordinary science. Your paragraph could make these points and supply instances of scenes where Michael takes on monstrous invulnerability. Another paragraph might be devoted to plot structure. Like many horror films, *Halloween* builds its plot around the monster's stalking and killing several characters; here, each of Michael's assaults replays the night he murdered his sister after she had sex with a local boy. This brings up the genre convention of punishing sexually active characters, a common element of 1980s horror (parodied in *Scream* and its follow-ups). A final paragraph could be devoted to the teenage Laurie, who seems to be a special target of Michael's stalking. Unlike her pals, Laurie is not sexually promiscuous, and she genuinely cares about the children she baby-sits for. As in many horror films (*King Kong*, *Nosferatu*), the pure beauty attracts the monster but also plays a role in his downfall.

The thrust of your screening report is descriptive. Instead of developing an original argument, you're showing how the assigned film is relevant to issues being examined in the course. By drawing on clear, powerful examples from your notes, your report can demonstrate not only that you've watched the film with understanding but that you are actively engaging with the broader ideas in class. The same skill at relating aspects of the movie to issues in the course will be helpful for you in writing essay examination answers.

---

### Key Questions for a Screening Report

1. Have you shown how the film is relevant to issues explored in the course or the specific assignment?
2. Have you displayed your familiarity with the whole film?
3. Have you confined yourself to one, two, or at most three aspects of the film, each one developed in a paragraph or two?
4. Have you drawn concrete examples from the film—shots, lines of dialogue, elements of plot or characterization—which support the aspects you've picked out?

## The Film Review

The screening report tends to be mainly descriptive, although you may be asked to express an opinion about what is interesting or valuable about the movie. The film review makes evaluation far more central. It is essentially a judgment about the quality of the movie, backed up with enough information to indicate that your judgment is based on good reasons. If you write for a campus newspaper or an online publication, your review will be devoted to a film currently playing in theatres, so you become a consumer adviser, trying to indicate whether the movie is worth buying a ticket for. "I look at films," says *Los Angeles Times* reviewer Kenneth Turan, "and I provide a point of view on them, for people who are trying to figure out if they want to see the movie or not" (*Projections* 10, ed. Mike Figgis [London: Faber and Faber, 2000], p. 61).

Professional reviewers like Turan are commonly known as film *critics*—a term which implies their commitment to making judgments. Yet even though many readers think that film critics are too tough on the movies they see, film criticism isn't devoted to finding fault. The best reviews aren't simply thumbs-up-thumbs-down opinions. For one thing, a good review avoids extreme judgments ("a thoroughly bad movie," "a flawless film"). Most good films aren't perfect, and many weak films have some good points. The sensitive critic tries to take both pluses and minuses into account.

Moreover, most critics recognize that not all readers have the same tastes. One reader might find *Titanic* thrillingly romantic, but another might find it slushy. So the review might offer something like this: "If you like shameless wallowing in old-fashioned rich-girl-poor-boy romance, you'll love *Titanic*. For me, a little schmaltz goes a long way."

This acknowledges that the reviewer is aware that the reader might actually enjoy the film that's about to be judged harshly. Readers quickly sense a critic's preferences and tend to follow critics whose tastes they trust to be like their own.

The film review is a genre of journalistic writing, and it depends on certain conventions. There must a brief plot synopsis, suggesting the main conflicts and character developments. Typically, however, the reviewer doesn't divulge the ending. The main characters' names are followed by actor's names in parentheses:

> Neo (Keanu Reeves) follows Trinity (Carrie-Anne Moss) down the rabbit hole into an adventure that calls the very existence of our world into question.
>
> —*The Matrix*

Reviewers are also expected to mention striking aspects of the film: impressive sets or costumes, notable visual qualities such as color design or cutting or music, and, above all, acting. Comments on these matters can be given separately or woven into the synopsis ("The hacker Neo, played by Keanu Reeves with his usual unflappably dazed look...."). Reviewers also compare the film at hand with other films which belong to the same genre, which are made by the same filmmaker, or which raise similar thematic issues. This convention demands that the critic be familiar with a wide range of films and some film history.

Perhaps the biggest constraint is brevity. The typical film review runs two to five pages, double-spaced—not a lot of room to develop a complex judgment of a movie. Newspaper critics labor under very tight space restrictions, although magazine critics tend to have more chance to develop their ideas. The most famous film critics, such as Graham Greene in the 1930s and André Bazin and François Truffaut in the 1940s and 1950s, wrote for weekly and monthly publications.

The best reviewers excel as writers. They render their opinions in short, memorable strokes. They devise arresting openings and pointed wrap-ups. To give the flavor of a movie, they aim at vivid descriptions. In a few words they can evoke the look and sound, even the emotional overtones, of a movie.  Here is Dwight Macdonald on *L'Avventura*:

> The sound track is a miracle. Instead of relying on "mood music," Antonioni uses everyday sounds, modulating and blending them to get his effects: the wash of waves, dogs barking, trains groaning and clicking along, the harsh confused sounds of a crowd, the panting breath of lovers. In the visit to the deserted town near Noto, silence prevails, punctuated finally by the slamming of the car doors as the baffled searchers drive away.
>
> (*On Movies* [Englewood Cliffs, N.J.: Prentice-Hall, 1969], p. 333)

When a critic wants to point out the defects in a movie, there is no room for a lengthy demolition job. A crisp killer line serves best, as when Pauline Kael's appraises Robert DeNiro's quiet, expressionless acting: "He could be a potato, except that he's thoroughly absorbed in the process of doing nothing" (*Taking It All In* [New York: Holt, Rinehart, & Winston, 1984], p. 241).

The reviewer may cultivate a highly personal style. Manny Farber is one of the most distinctive voices in English-language film criticism, mixing tough-guy cynicism with an eye for precise visuals:

There is a half-minute bit in *Twelve Angry Men* in which the halo-wearing minority vote on the jury, a pinch-faced architect (Henry Fonda), is seen carefully drying each fingernail with a bathroom towel. It is a sharply effective, stalling-for-time type of adverse detailing, showing the jury's one sensitive, thoughtful figure to be unusually prissy. Unfortunately, this mild debunking of the hero is a coldly achieved detail that sits on the surface of the film, unexplored and unimportant.

(*Negative Space: Manny Farber on the Movies* [New York: Da Capo, 1998], p. 122).

Macdonald, Kael, Farber, Andrew Sarris, Phillip Lopate, Vernon Young, and other critics have published collections of their film reviews, and these are worth studying as pieces of careful writing. To get a sense of current reviewing practice, you can examine reviews by Todd McCarthy (*Variety*), Andrew Sarris (*The New York Observer*), J. Hoberman and Amy Taubin (*The Village Voice*), Armond White (*The New York Press*), Elvis Mitchell (*The New York Times*), Richard Corliss (*Time*), Roger Ebert (*The Chicago Sun-Times*), Michael Wilmington (*The Chicago Tribune*), Jonathan Rosenbaum (*The Chicago Reader*), Manohla Dargis (*LA Weekly*), Owen Glieberman (*Entertainment Weekly*), Geoff Andrew (*Time Out*, London), and Philip French (*The Observer*, London). Some publications file reviews on their websites. Longer reviews are published in *Film Comment* and *Cineaste* (New York), *Film Quarterly* (Berkeley), *Sight & Sound* (London), *Cinema Papers* (Victoria, Australia), *24 Images* (Montreal), and *CinemaScope* (Toronto).

---

### Key Questions for a Film Review

1. Have you somewhere clearly indicated your judgment of the film's quality?
2. Have you provided a brief plot synopsis?
3. Have you mentioned specific elements of the film which support your judgment? Have you described these quickly and vividly, using concrete language and metaphors?
4. Have you qualified your judgment by balancing positive and negative aspects of the film?
5. Have you begun the review with an attention-grabbing opening? Have you concluded it with a striking sentence?

# An Analytical Essay

The analytical film essay typically runs 5 to 15 double-spaced pages. Being an analysis, it points out how various parts of the film fit together systematically (see *Film Art*, p. 351). Like a screening report and a review, the analytical essay includes descriptions, but the descriptions are typically more detailed and extensive. Like the review, the analytical essay also puts forth the writer's opinion, but here the opinion doesn't usually address the ultimate worth of the film. When you analyze a film, you're defending your view of the ways parts of the movie work together.

Think about a sad song. You could *describe* the song in various ways ("It's about a woman who wants out of a dead-end relationship"). You could also give your *evaluation* of it ("It's too sentimental"). But you can also *analyze* it, talking about how the lyrics, the melody, and the instrumentation work together to create the feeling of sadness or to make the listener understand the relationship. That's the sort of thing people who study film do when they analyze movies.

The analytical essay is also an *argumentative* piece. Its goal is to allow you to develop an idea you have about the film by supplying good reasons for considering that idea seriously. The sample analyses in Chapter 11 are argumentative essays. For instance, in analyzing *The Thin Blue Line*, we argue that the film tells a real-life story in a way that suggests how difficult the search for truth can be (pp. 380–381). Likewise, our discussion of *Raging Bull* tries to show that the film criticizes violence as used in mass entertainment while still displaying a fascination with its visceral appeal (p. 392).

## Preparing to Write

How do you come up with an argument for your essay? The preparatory work usually consists of three steps.

### 1. Develop a *thesis* which your essay will explain and support

Start by asking yourself questions. What do you find intriguing or disturbing about the film? What makes the film noteworthy, in your opinion? Does it illustrate some aspect of filmmaking with special clarity? Does it have an unusual effect on the viewer? Do its implicit or symptomatic meanings seem to have particular importance?

Your answer to such questions will furnish the *thesis* of your analysis. The thesis, in any piece of writing, is the central claim your argument advances. It encapsulates your opinion, but not in the way that a film review states your evaluation of the movie. In an analytical essay, your thesis is one way to help other viewers understand the movie. In our analysis of *His Girl Friday* (pp. 352–356), our thesis is that the film uses classical narrative devices to create an impression of rapid speed. With respect to *Man with a Movie Camera* (pp. 376–380), our thesis is that the film makes the viewer aware of how even documentary films manipulate the world they present to us.

Typically, your thesis will be a claim about the film's *functions*, its *effects*, or its *meanings* (or some mixture of all three). For instance, we argue that by creating a wide variety of characters in *Do The Right Thing,* Spike Lee builds up interconnected plotlines; this allows him to explore the problems of maintaining a community (pp. 361–366). In our discussion of *North by Northwest*, we concentrate more on how the film achieves the effects of suspense and surprise (pp. 356–361). The analysis of *Meet Me in St. Louis* emphasizes how technique carries implicit and symptomatic meanings about the importance of family life in America (pp. 387–389).

Your thesis will need some support, some reasons to believe it. Ask yourself, "What would back up my thesis?" and draw up a list of points. Some of these reasons will occur to you immediately, but others will emerge only as you start to study the film more closely. And the reasons, which are conceptual points, will in turn need backup—typically, evidence and examples. You can sum up the structure of an argumentative essay in the acronym **TREE**: **Thesis** supported by **Reasons** which rest upon **Evidence** and **Examples**.

## 2. Draw up a segmentation of the entire film

Analyzing a film is a bit like understanding a building's design. When we walk through a building, we notice various features—the shape of a doorway, the sudden appearance of an immense atrium. We may not, however, have a very strong sense of the building's overall architecture. If we are students of architecture, though, we want to study the design of the whole building, and so we'd examine the blueprints to understand how all the individual parts fit together. Similarly, we experience a film scene by scene, but if we want to understand how the various scenes work together, it's helpful to have a sense of the whole film's shape.

Movies don't come equipped with blueprints, so we have to make our own. The best way to grasp the overall shape of the movie is to make a segmentation, as we suggest in *Film Art*. (See in particular pp. 55, 80, 116–117, 124, 132, and 139.) Breaking the film into sequences gives you a convenient overview, and your segmentation will often suggest things that will support or help you nail down your thesis. For example, in studying *The Thin Blue Line*, we made a separate list of all the flashbacks to the murder. When we saw them lined up on our page, we spotted the pattern of development in them which became part of our analysis (pp. 381–382).

Now that you have a segmentation, you can go on to see how the parts are connected. In examining a nonnarrative film, you will need to be especially alert to its use of categorical, rhetorical, abstract, or assoc-iational principles. See our analysis of *Gap-Toothed Women* (pp. 116-122) for an example of how you can base an analysis on the overall shape of the film.

If the film presents a narrative, your segmentation can help you answer questions like these: How does each scene set up causes and effects? At what point do we understand the characters' goals, and how do those goals develop in the course of the action? What principles of development connect one scene to another? The opening scenes of *Jerry Maguire* establish Jerry as a sports agent who's having a crisis of conscience. Fearing he's becoming "another shark in a suit," he impulsively sends out a memo (what he calls a "mission statement") that criticizes his firm's policies. Because of his insubordination, he's fired. Because he needs a job, he tries to build his independent agency on trust, but he sometimes falls back into taking his clients for granted. The bulk of the film consists of his struggle to remain principled—with the help of a woman who tries to bring out his better side and a player who tries to teach him the value of direct communication. Thus the romantic plot line develops in relation to Jerry's efforts to improve both his business and his personality. An analysis of the narrative would show how each scene continues the cause-effect logic, affects the hero's goals, and traces out the changes in his character and his love life.

Should you include your segmentation in your written analysis? Sometimes it will make your argument clearer and more convincing. We think that a broad scene breakdown helps illustrate some key points in our discussions of *His Girl Friday* (p. 353) and a more detailed one clarifies *The Thin Blue Line* (pp. 381–382). Perhaps your argument will gain in strength if you bring out a still finer-grained segmentation; we do this in considering the three subsegments of the final chase scene in *North by Northwest* (pp. 359–361).

However much of your segmentation finally surfaces in your written analysis, it's good to get in the habit of writing out a fairly detailed segmentation every time you examine a film.  It will help you get an overall sense of the film's design. You probably noticed that nearly every one of our analyses includes, early on, a statement about the film's underlying formal organization.  This provides a firm basis for more detailed analysis. Writing out a segmentation is also good practice if you want to become a filmmaker yourself: screenwriters, directors, and other creative personnel usually work from a plot outline that amounts to a segmentation.

## 3. Note outstanding instances of film technique

As you watch the film, you should jot down brief, accurate descriptions of various film techniques that are used.  You can get ideas for analyzing style from Chapter 10.  Once you have determined the overall organizational structure of the film, you can identify salient techniques, trace out patterns of techniques across the whole film, and propose functions for those techniques. These techniques will often support or refine your thesis.

Most basically, you should be alert for techniques taken one by one. Is this a case of three-point lighting? Is this a continuity cut?  Just as important, the analyst should be sensitive to context: What is the function of the technique *here*? Again a segmentation will help you by drawing attention to patterning. Does the technique repeat or develop across the film?

At any moment in a film, so much is going on that it's easy to be overwhelmed by all the technical elements. Shot composition, performance, lighting, camera movement, color design, dialogue, music—all these things can be present and changing from second to second. Often, beginning film analysts are uncertain as to what techniques are most relevant to their thesis.  Sometimes they try to describe every single costume or cut or pan, and they wind up drowned in data.

This is where planning your paper's thesis in advance helps you.  Your thesis will make certain techniques more pertinent than others.  For example, we argue that in *North by Northwest* Hitchcock creates suspense and surprise by manipulating our range of knowledge (pp. 356–361). Sometimes he lets us know more than the main character, Roger Thornhill, and this builds up suspense: Will Thornhill walk into the traps that we know are awaiting him? At other moments we know only as much as Thornhill does, so that we're as surprised as he is at a new turn of events. Hitchcock devotes particular film techniques to creating these effects. Crosscutting between lines of action gives us more knowledge than Thornhill has, while POV camerawork and cutting restrict us to his understanding of certain situations.

So other techniques, such as lighting or performance style, aren't as relevant to our thesis about *North by Northwest*. (They might, however, be very relevant to some other thesis about it—say, that it treats thriller conventions somewhat comically.) By contrast, we emphasize acting technique somewhat more in our discussion of *Raging Bull*, because acting is pertinent to our discussion of the film's use of realistic conventions. Similarly, the editing in *Meet Me in St. Louis* would be interesting from the standpoint of another argument, but it is not central to the one that we are making, so it goes almost completely unmentioned.

Once you have a thesis, an awareness of the overall shape of the film, and a set of notes on the techniques relevant to your thesis, you are ready to organize your analytical paper.

## Organization and Writing

Broadly speaking, an argumentative piece has this underlying structure:

**Introduction:**  Background information or a vivid example, leading up to:
*Statement of thesis*
**Body:**  Reasons to believe the thesis
Evidence and examples that support the thesis
**Conclusion:**  Restatement of thesis and discussion of its broader implications

All of our analyses in Chapter 11 adhere to this basic structure. The opening portion seeks to lead the reader into the argument to come, and the thesis is introduced at the end of this introduction. Where the introduction is brief, as in the *His Girl Friday* analysis, the thesis comes at the end of the first paragraph (pp. 352–353). Where more background material is needed, the introduction is somewhat longer and the thesis is stated a little later. In the *Thin Blue Line* essay, the thesis comes at the end of the third paragraph (pp. 380–381).

As you know, the building block of any piece of writing is the paragraph. Each slot in the argumentative pattern outlined above will be filled by one or more paragraphs. The introduction is at least one paragraph, the body will be several paragraphs, and the conclusion will be one or two paragraphs.

Typically, the introductory paragraphs of a film analysis don't display much concrete evidence. Instead, this is the place to introduce the thesis you want to advance. Often this involves situating the thesis in relation to some background information. For example, our analysis of *Tokyo Story* situates the film in a tradition of noncontinuity editing before stating our thesis (p. 371). Usually the introductory paragraph or two set out generalizations of this sort.

If you're adventurous, however, you may wish to avoid background information. You can start with one concrete piece of evidence—say, an intriguing scene or detail from the film—before you move quickly to state your thesis. Our *Meet Me in St. Louis* piece uses this sort of opening (p. 386).

Writing a film analysis poses a particular problem of organization. Should the body of the argument follow the film's progress in chronological order, so that each paragraph deals with a scene or major part? In some cases this can work. We try it with our *Gap-Toothed Women* discussion, which traces out the patterns of development across the film (pp. 116–122). By and large, however, you strengthen your argument by following a more conceptual structure of the sort indicated in our outline.

The body of your essay consists of a series of *reasons* to believe the thesis. You'll back those points up with evidence and examples. Consider our analysis of *Breathless* (pp. 366–371). Our thesis is that Godard's film both pays homage to *film noir* outlaw movies and reworks their conventions through a rough-edged treatment. This thesis obliges us to use a comparison-and-contrast strategy. But first we start with a paragraph of background (p. 366), sketching the relevant Hollywood outlaw-movie traditions. The second paragraph (pp. 366–367) shows how the basic story of *Breathless* resembles the criminal-couple-on-the-run movie. The next three paragraphs (p. 367) make the point that Godard's film also reworks Hollywood conventions: Michel seems to be imitating tough-guy stars, while the film's form and style seem casual, as if aiming to let the audience enjoy a new, more self-conscious version of an American crime movie.

Since the essay relies on comparison and contrast, the body of the piece explores the film's similarities to and differences from Hollywood conventions. The next eleven paragraphs seek to establish these points about the film's narrative form:

1. Michel is like a Hollywood protagonist in certain ways (p. 367).

**2.**  The action is, however, much more choppy and digressive than in a Hollywood film (p. 367).

**3.**  The death of the policeman is handled more abruptly and disconcertingly than in a normal action movie (p. 367).

**4., 5.**  By contrast, the bedroom conversation of Patricia and Michel is untypical of Hollywood genre scenes because it is very static, marking little progress toward Michel's goals (pp. 367–368).

**6.**  Once the plot starts moving again, it stalls again (p. 368).

**7., 8.**  Moving toward resolution, the plot again picks up, but the finale remains enigmatic and open-ended (p. 368).

**9., 10.**  Overall, Michel and Patricia are puzzling and hard to read as characters (p. 368–369).

**11.**  The characterization of the couple is thus sharply different from that of the romantic couple in most outlaws-on-the-run plots (p. 369).

Each of these points constitutes a reason to accept the thesis that *Breathless* uses genre conventions but also revises them in unsettling ways.

Supporting reasons may be of many sorts. Several of our analyses distinguish between reasons based upon the film's overall narrative form and reasons based upon stylistic choices. The portion of the *Breathless* essay we've just reviewed offers evidence to support our claims about the film's reworking of Hollywood narrative conventions. The paragraphs that follow this material (pp. 369–371) discuss Godard's similarly self-conscious use of stylistic strategies. In analyzing *Meet Me in St. Louis,* we concentrate more on reviewing various motifs that create particular thematic effects. In either case, the argument rests on a thesis, supported by reasons, which are in turn supported by evidence and examples.

If you organize the essay conceptually rather than as a blow-by-blow résumé of the action, you may find it useful to acquaint your reader with the plot action at some point. A brief synopsis soon after the introduction may do the trick. (See, for example, our *North by Northwest* analysis, pp. 356–361.) Alternatively, you may wish to cover basic plot material when you discuss segmentation, characterization, causal progression, or other topics. The crucial point is that the writer isn't forced to follow the film's order.

Typically, each reason for the thesis becomes the topic sentence of a paragraph, with more detailed evidence displayed in the sentences that follow. In the *Breathless* example, each main point is followed by specific examples of how plot action, dialogue, or film techniques at once refer to Hollywood tradition and loosen up the conventions. Here is where your detailed notes about salient scenes or techniques will be very useful. You can select the strongest and most vivid instances of mise-en-scene, cinematography, editing, and sound to back up the main point that each paragraph explores.

The body of the analysis can be made more persuasive by several other tactics. A paragraph that compares or contrasts this film with another might help you zero in on specific aspects that are central to your argument. You can also include a brief in-depth analysis of a single scene or sequence that drives your argumentative point home. We use this tactic in discussing several films' endings, chiefly because a concluding section often reveals broad principles of development. For instance, the last two scenes of *Jerry Maguire* underscore the two plotlines, professional and personal. First comes his professional reward: Jerry's client Rod triumphs on the field and pays tribute to Jerry's personal investment in his career. The last scene shows Jerry, Dorothy, and her son strolling past a playground, underscoring their reconciliation as a family (and developing the hints dropped in the beginning that one of Jerry's redeeming qualities is his concern for children). Just as we advise you to pay particular attention to the film's ending as a key place to discover what the film's trying to do (p. 55), a close analysis of the film's ending can be a convincing way to end the body of your analysis.

In general, the body of the argument should progress toward stronger or subtler reasons for believing the thesis. In discussing *The Thin Blue Line*, we start by tracing how the film provides a kind of reconstructed investigation, leading to the killer (pp. 380–383). Only then do we ask: Is the film more than a neutral report of the case (383–384)? This leads us to argue that the filmmaker has subtly aligned our sympathies with Randall Adams (p. 384). Yet the film goes beyond aligning us with Adams. It also bombards us with a great deal of information, some of it fairly minute, even trivial. The purpose, we suggest, is to make the viewers share some of the obligation to sort out conflicting data and notice apparently minor details (pp. 384–385). This is a fairly complex point that would probably not come across if introduced early on. Only after the analysis has worked through more clear-cut matters is it possible to consider such nuances of interpretation.

How to end your argumentative essay? Now is the time to restate the thesis (skillfully, not repeating previous statements word for word) and to remind the reader of the reasons to entertain the thesis. The ending is also an opportunity for you to try for a bit of eloquence, a telling quotation, a bit of historical context, or a concrete motif from the film itself—perhaps a line of dialogue or an image that encapsulates your thesis. In making preparatory notes, ask yourself constantly: Is there something here that can create a vivid ending?

Just as there is no general recipe for understanding film, there is no formula for writing incisive and enlightening film analyses. But there are principles and rules of thumb that govern good writing of all sorts. Only through writing, and constant rewriting, do these principles and rules come to seem second nature. By analyzing films, we can understand the sources of our pleasure in them and we are able to share that understanding with others. If we succeed, the writing itself can give pleasure to ourselves and our readers.

---

### Key Questions for an Analytical Essay

1. Do you have a thesis? Is it stated clearly by the end of the first or second paragraph of your analysis?
2. Do you have a series of reasons supporting the thesis? Are these arranged in logical and convincing order (with the strongest reason coming last)?
3. Are your supporting reasons backed up? Do your segmentation and your stylistic analysis provide specific evidence and examples for each reason you offer?
4. Does your beginning orient your reader to the direction of your argument? Does your concluding paragraph reiterate your thesis and provide a vivid ending?

## A Sample Analytical Essay

The following paper was written by a sophomore for an introductory film course. The assignment asked for an analytical essay on Martin Scorsese's *King of Comedy*, concentrating on two or three scenes of particular importance to the paper's thesis. A segmentation of the film (not included here) was attached.

Note how the essay begins with some general observations and then focuses its thesis in the second paragraph. In order to trace the greater blurring of fantasy and reality in the film, the author develops a strategy of comparison and contrast. Each paragraph develops specific evidence of the various techniques Scorsese uses, considering editing, sound, camerawork, and staging. The paper concludes by speculating on how these techniques affect the viewer and reinforce one of the film's themes. A crisp summary line drives home the main thesis: "Our final image of Rupert may be an image of the man or it may be an image from the man."

### Fantasy and Reality in *The King of Comedy*
by Amanda Robillard

America is obsessed with fame. Television shows and magazines have been created in order to let the masses delve into the personal lives of their favorite stars. Friends gossip about people they have never met, but whom they feel they know because of the mass media. The lives of celebrities may not be perfect, but they definitely are exciting. Learning about your favorite star's life is an entertaining escape from what can seem a mundane existence.

Fame becomes alluring because a fantasy world surrounds it. Martin Scorsese's film *The King of Comedy* focuses on Rupert Pupkin's obsession with fame. Not only is he obsessed with a famous comedian, but he is consumed with becoming a famous comedian himself and comes to believe that his idol is more than willing to help him in his quest. Pupkin's obsession goes beyond a mere interest in fame; it takes over his life to the point that he can no longer distinguish reality from the fantasies he has concocted. Because the viewer is allowed to see these fantasies through Rupert's eyes, one can track his progression further and further into his fantasy world. In *The King of Comedy*, Scorsese uses various aspects of style in order to manipulate the boundaries between fantasy and reality in such a way as to draw a parallel between Rupert's progressive withdrawal into his own fantasies and the viewer's inability to tell the difference between the two.

The first fantasy scene of *The King of Comedy*, segment number three, blurs the line between fantasy and reality, but the line is nonetheless still discernible. Here Scorsese uses aspects of style to create a coherent fantasy that is easily recognizable as such. It is distinctly separate from surrounding scenes of reality while at the same time drawing on them in order to create the fantasy.

A combined use of sound and editing is used to tie the fantasy to reality. This is apparent both in the scenes that surround segment three and within the scene itself. Rupert invited Jerry to lunch at the end of segment two. This invitation leads into a shot of Jerry and Rupert seated in a restaurant in the following scene. This link from actual dialogue to fantasy is a continuing pattern throughout the film, brought out by first mentioning the act in a real conversation and then having it carried out in a fantasy later in the film. Editing the scenes together in such a way is one device used to blur the distinction between fantasy and reality.

Within the scene, juxtaposing Rupert's fantasy with his acting it out in his mother's basement serves to create a distinction between the two. Sometimes reverse-shots of Rupert show him dressed for the lunch; at other moments, the reverse-shots show him in his basement, dressed differently. Similarly, while still seeing an image of Jerry and Rupert eating lunch together in a restaurant, we hear Rupert's mother yelling for him to keep quiet or inquiring whom he is talking to. The editing and sound techniques guide the viewer back into reality, where Rupert is actually enacting the fantasy in his basement. Again, however, some elements carry over between fantasy and reality. Photographs behind Jerry in the fantasy are echoed by photographs on the wall behind Rupert in his basement. Jerry also happens to be wearing the same shirt and tie that he had in the previous scene, although with a different jacket. Also, the source of lighting seems to be coming from Rupert's right in both fantasy and reality, although it is softer in the shots in his basement.

All of these elements of style serve to connect fantasy to reality while at the same time drawing definite distinctions between the two. Similarities are needed in order to create a believable fantasy that Rupert would feasibly have at the time. Drawing on these similarities allows the viewer to notice patterns that develop across the course of the film, and the variations in these patterns serve to steadily blur the line between fantasy and reality even further with each fantasy sequence. At this point in the film, there are still enough differences between the two realms to clearly separate the two from each other. This is true for Rupert—as he acts out the two roles of his fantasy, he is distinctly aware that the events are not actually happening to him—as well as for the viewer, who is provided with subjective fantasy shots as well as shots of Rupert's sad reality and enough stylistic clues to separate what is really happening from what Rupert would like to happen.

One of Rupert's later fantasies, in segment fifteen, marks a further progression into the fantasy world. Rupert's mind is no longer occupied by simple matters like having a lunch date with his idol. Instead, he now dreams of receiving, all at the same time, everything he could possibly imagine wanting: a spot on the Jerry Langford Show, fame, apologies for every wrong ever done to him, and the love of his life becoming his wife while millions of people watch. Rupert's fantasies have become much more complicated as he gets more and more obsessed with becoming a famous comedian with the help of Jerry Langford.

These more intricate fantasies require a bolder use of style. Because Rupert is becoming ever more wrapped up in his world of make-believe, the added time he spends dreaming up this world allows for more special effects. Sound and editing are once again used to blur Rupert's reality and his imagination. It should be noted that this fantasy sequence is sandwiched between two framing sequences of Rupert in the offices of the Jerry Langford Show, waiting to see what they thought of his tape.

This fantasy is not a distinct unit in and of itself, as the first one was, but instead a scene firmly entrenched in the scene surrounding it. An entire phrase is uttered from the fantasy while the image track still shows Rupert looking around the office. Also, this fantasy takes place in the same place where Rupert's body is really located at the time of his mind's wanderings. Granted, one is in the studio and the other in the office, but they are both in the same building, unlike the earlier restaurant/basement segment.

Style is also a crucial element in the portrayal of this fantasy. Rupert imagines this scene as if it were on television. The fuzzy picture and the tinny sound of the dialogue serve to suggest this medium. Characters in the fantasy also present themselves directly to the camera. The set design of the show is the same as that really used on Jerry's show. The more complicated subject matter of this fantasy is portrayed using more complicated cinematography and editing. Throughout most of the movie, editing is made to go unnoticed. However, in this scene many steps are taken to make sure the editing and camerawork are noticed. An extreme close-up of the piano player's hands zooms out to a shot of him and the piano, before panning up and left as it dissolves into a shot of Rita, and then continues to pan left as she makes her way to Rupert.

Here the image zooms out to a long shot of the couple before dissolving into a close-up of Rupert and Rita. This is by far the most complicated sequence in the film, a film which otherwise consists mostly of invisible editing. These stylistic elements are meant to be noticed. They serve as an illustration of Rupert's more complicated fantasy world, a world which is becoming ever more real to him.

Although it would seem that this fantasy world is becoming increasingly more important to Rupert, the viewer is still aware of the sequence as a fantasy, but through fewer cues this time. Gone are the blatant juxtapositions between the two worlds and the interruptions of fantasy by reality. Rupert is no longer shown acting out both roles in his fantasy. A single voice, that of Dr. Joyce Brothers, sounds unnatural, as if a man were impersonating the higher pitch of a woman's voice. Within the scene, this is the only sonic betrayal of reality, and it can only be heard if one pays close attention. However, the intricate camera movements and editing used to show Rupert's appearance on the Jerry Langford Show also serve to distinctly mark it as a fantasy. It is far more complex than anything seen in any reality segments and thus must be taken to be fantasy.

Although the viewer can tell that this segment is fantasy, it is exponentially more complicated than previous segments and thus also serves to show Rupert's withdrawal further from reality. If the first fantasy segment was one in which the line between fantasy and reality was blurred but still distinctly there, this segment serves to blur the line even further, so that the line is no longer as clear as it once had been. This segment is an integral part in the process of a complete loss of anything separating reality from fantasy, both for Rupert and for the viewer.

The final segment of *The King of Comedy* is such a segment. Nothing can be said for certain as to whether it is reality or fantasy. The ending is left ambiguous. The two have become completely blurred so that the question of reality or fantasy is left in the hands of the viewer, with just enough stylistic and narrative prodding to leave you second-guessing yourself no matter what decision you make. At first glance the scene can be dismissed as reality, but a second look clearly identifies it as fantasy. A third, and you're no longer sure exactly what it is. Even if you think it is one or the other, there is still an inkling of doubt that refuses to be ignored and causes you to wonder. Scorsese doesn't hand over a clear and concise ending to top this film off but instead forces the viewer to earn it.

Most of this segment (number twenty-nine) could be interpreted as simply Rupert's fantasy of achieving fame, but that would be premature. While its elements may not be completely compatible with reality, they don't blend completely with fantasy either. For example, the segment begins with an announcer's voice telling of Rupert Pupkin's outrageous debut on the Jerry Langford Show. This voice is heard first over a black screen. The image is soon replaced by "file tape" from news reports. Was this sound bridge from black to footage meant to be a bridge from reality to fantasy, as the previous ones had been? Or is it meant to separate this segment from the rest of the film so as to be taken as a lapse in time between Rupert's arrest and his rise to fame? The "file tape" label creates a sense of reality, whereas the flamboyant nature of the announcer does the opposite by creating what Rupert would surely believe to be the perfect soundbite. The grainy television image also brings up questions of reality versus fantasy. Is it reminiscent of the television appearance Rupert made in his third fantasy segment? Or is it instead actually footage from his monologue on the Jerry Langford Show being rebroadcast on different news channels?

In either case, the panning, zooming, and craning of the camera over the magazine headlines and book displays all call to mind the wedding-fantasy sequence. However, the number of headlines present is hard to believe as the workings of a single man's thoughts. And, given the nature of fame in our culture, isn't it likely that Rupert would receive book and movie offers as a "reward" for his kidnapping of Jerry?

Still, interpretation is then left swinging back toward fantasy when one notices that the news reports never mention his accomplice, Masha. Is this because Masha's involvement was really deemed too inconsequential by the press? It seems more likely that her absence here would arise from Rupert's obvious disdain for her. In his fantasy he would be likely to erase Masha from any involvement in the plan.

The final shot of *The King of Comedy* does little to resolve these issues and instead serves to complicate them further. This shot begins as a high angle and cranes down and in so as to get closer and closer to Rupert's figure standing in the spotlight on stage as an announcer continues to describe him as a success and the crowd cheers. The lengthy take and the announcer's repetition of Rupert's name, along with the applause that ceases to die down, could suggest that we are now definitely in Rupert's mind, as he prolongs his moment of triumph. Yet the shot is very similar to others we've seen on Jerry's show, and we cannot rule out the possibility that in today's celebrity culture Rupert has indeed achieved his goal of becoming a famous comedian. After all, the real audience for Jerry's show did seem to enjoy Rupert's rather lame jokes.

The fact that this final segment cannot simply be dismissed as fantasy serves to illustrate the fact that Scorsese successfully built up narrative and stylistic elements in his fantasy sequences so as to blur their distinction from each other. Each fantasy remains dependent on the previous reality and fantasy scenes so as to be distinguishable as such. As Rupert's obsession with becoming famous grows, so too does his fantasy world. As his fantasies grow, they become more entrenched in reality and thus more plausible to the viewer. Our final image of Rupert may be an image of the man or it may be an image from the man. Perhaps Rupert ends up only being successful at his craft in his fantasy world, but Martin Scorsese definitely manipulated stylistic elements of *The King of Comedy* to successfully craft a film in which the line between fantasy and reality is blurred not only for the character but for the viewer as well.

 # Writing Resources

## Library Sources

The Notes and Queries section at the end of each chapter of *Film Art* points you toward books and articles which can help you learn more about the topics covered. In addition, here are some general library reference works you should be acquainted with.

For a thorough dictionary of terms, see Ira Konigsberg, *The Complete Film Dictionary*, 2d ed. (New York: Penguin, 1997). Also very useful is Ephraim Katz, *The Film Encyclopedia*, 2d ed. (New York: Harper, 1994). Both of these are available in reasonably priced paperback editions.

When you want to find articles about a film subject, turn to two annual indexes which most college libraries hold: *The Film Literature Index* (Albany: Albany Filmdex, Inc., 1999) and *The International Index of Film Periodicals* (Copenhagen: FIAF). These can help you find articles by film, director, genre, topic, and author. Older but still useful sources are Richard Dyer MacCann and Edward S. Perry, eds., *The New Film Index* (New York: E. P. Dutton, 1975), which surveys English-language articles between 1930 and 1970; and John C. Gerlach and Lana

Gerlach, *The Critical Index* (New York: Teachers College Press, 1974), which covers articles in English from 1946 to 1973. Film reviews are reprinted in *Film Review Annual* (Englewood, N.J.: Jerome S. Ozer).

## The Internet

There is a remarkable amount of information about cinema available online. The Web is so dazzling a resource that we tend to forget its drawbacks. For one thing, its information is ephemeral; a website may vanish overnight. Moreover, material published in books, magazines, newspapers, and scholarly journals has to be reviewed for accuracy and reliability, but a webpage can assert anything, no matter how fanciful or unreliable.

When appraising Web-derived information, ask yourself: Who is the author? Is the host a reliable site? Is the information current and objective? Is it designed to promote or sell a product? Is the author presenting information in order to inform readers, or is there another agenda at work? When possible, you should verify the information with other sources, both Web-based and print-based. These questions are explored in Moira Anderson Allen, *writing.com* (New York: Allworth, 1999), pp. 22-23.

Web resources come in many shapes. A **search engine**, such as AltaVista, Infoseek, and HotBot, allows you to search websites by keywords. If you want information on Steven Spielberg, a search engine will locate fansites devoted to him, as well as sites established by film companies to promote particular Spielberg films. There are meta-search engines such as <mamma.com>, <www.dogpile.com>, and <www.metafind.com> . A guide to using search engines is found at Best Information on the Net <www.sau.edu/bestinfo/index.htm> . See also <www.marylaine.com>. It's always advisable to try several search engines on a given topic, since each one may bring up quite different sources. There are also **directories**, like Yahoo!, which are more selective but less comprehensive than search engines. A directory of directories is All-in-One Search Page <www.allonesearch.com>.

Most search engines do not search **databases**, which are compilations of information—statistics, official records, bibliographies, and encyclopedias. There are several university sites which supply access to databases. Try as well Direct Search <gwis2.circ.gwu.edu/~gprice/direct.htm> and My Virtual Reference Desk <www.refdesk.com> The most important name and title databases are the Internet Movie Database <us.imdb.com/a2z>and Film Index International

<www.lib.utexas.edu/Pubs/guides/chadwickhealey/filmch.html>, which lists credits for 90,000 films since 1930.

A **clearinghouse** selects and assembles information on a specific topic. Clearinghouses are usually created by people with solid knowledge of the subject, and they often include links to the best websites. A good general clearinghouse for film studies is Screensite: Film & TV Studies <www.sa.ua.edu/TCF/welcome.html >.   An example of a more specialized clearinghouse is Schauwecher's Guide to Japan: Movies <http://www.japan-guide.com/e/e2079.html>.

For more websites, see *Film Art,* pp. 435–436, and our Website <www.mhhe.com/filmart>. For help on Web-based research, try the excellent tutorial Finding Information on the Internet <www.lib.berkeley.edu/TeachingLib/Guides/ Internet/Findinfo.html>.